Susan Clements

Rambles in the Belfast Hills

Walking the Hills, Rivers and Shores of Belfast

First published by Cottage Publications,
an imprint of Laurel Cottage Ltd.
Ballyhay, Donaghadee, N. Ireland 2014.

Design & origination in N. Ireland.
Printed & bound in China.
ISBN 978 1 900935 95 1

Contents

Introduction

It's surprising how often we don't look at what's on our doorstep. Many times I have travelled miles to find an interesting walk, ignoring my local patch in the search for something different or challenging. When I first started exploring the Cave Hill I began to realise that when I decided to be a 'tourist at home' I saw things with new eyes.

With this in mind I set forth on my mission to persuade others to venture away from the rut and look around them. So some of the walks in this book may be familiar but approached from another angle or can be linked to other walks to make a longer distance challenge.

Another theme which came out of this was the idea of a circuit of walks round Belfast, again many of which can be linked to others by short road sections. I wanted to include a variety of environments, from the rugged countryside of Divis and Cave Hill to the more urban and city areas along the Lagan and Lough Shore. Where possible I tied in access to public transport at the ends of walks, especially for the linear ones.

Although the walks are close to the city some of them are on rugged upland terrain where conditions can change quickly so proper outdoor gear is advisable.

Belfast is a city surrounded and defined by hills and water. Everywhere you will see one or the other, or both, if you look beyond the obvious. So why not go on an 'adventure holiday' from your front door and see what you can find?

Samson and Goliath just visible across the Lough

Valley Park to Whiteabbey

Start: Valley Leisure Centre car park on Church Road
Finish: Whiteabbey village
Distance: About 5.5km/3.5 miles one way
Type of walk: All surfaced path
Car: Park at Valley Leisure Centre
Public transport: Metro 2D to Leisure Centre, Ulsterbus 163/563 or Metro 2G to Whiteabbey. Newtownabbey Town Service 367 runs infrequently between start and finish points.

Well fed birds on the Valley Park lake

Combining woods and seashore, this pleasant walk begins at the car park in front of the Valley Leisure Centre on Church Road. A wooden walkway at the rear or the car park leads you on round the end of the lake, a popular place for wild fowl with a pair of swans regularly nesting on the island in the middle.

Through the gate follow the main drive down to another entrance to the Valley Park, then cross the road to pass into the Glas na Bradan or Bradan Glen via the fancy stone gateway.

Entrance to Bradan Glen

The little river was used during the eighteenth century to power what was one of the first water-powered cotton mills in the country. It was built by Lancashire man Nicholas Grimshaw in the Mill Road area and water from the Glas na Bradan river, a more substantial waterway in those days and an important boundary, was diverted to supply the mill race.

Ramsons beside the path

A tarmac path meanders beside the river past housing and down through the woods; keeping on the right of the water you can enjoy the birdsong and dappled shade in this haven sandwiched between Rathcoole housing estate and Merville Garden Village on the far side of the river.

The brainchild of builder Thomas McGrath this was the first garden village to be constructed in Northern Ireland when it was completed in 1950. It was built in the grounds of Merville House, originally the estate of prominent banker John Brown and later occupied by Sir Edward Coey who in 1861 became the only Mayor of Belfast from the Liberal Party. The mansion was used for local government offices during the 1950's and more recently has been restored for use as an amenity for the local community. It's good to see a handsome old house like this being employed for something, rather than being torn down and replaced by a characterless block.

Although you are close to a busy shopping centre, on this side of the river you are hardly aware of it as you saunter along. In spring either side of the path is a froth of white Ramson flowers beneath the Sycamore trees.

As the path nears the busy Shore Road I usually go up the road a bit to make use of a traffic island to cross before heading under the railway bridge into Whitehouse Park. Just round the corner to the left is the 400 year old White House itself, though it has weathered back to the stones and it's no longer white. After suitable restoration this is now open most afternoons with audio visual displays themed round the arrival of William's army, which passed this way. The events are shown in a European context and it all makes for a really entertaining place to visit if you are at all interested in history.

The White House – not very white but worth a visit!

To continue your walk turn into the path past a small car park beside the lagoon, as it is rather optimistically called, created when the M5 partially cut off this bit of the lough and quite a good spot for wading birds, especially when the tide is out.

This brings you alongside Gideon's Green (named after a Huguenot diarist who came over with the army of William of Orange) and under a motorway bridge to the path along the shore. A right turn would take you towards the city along the cycle path which connects with a route

The lagoon, an attractive spot for birds

A chance to get down onto the sand

round the docks and all the way to Lisburn, – good for cycling but the section through the industrial estate at Duncrue makes it less attractive for walkers. Horizontal openings have been left in the fence at a couple of places along here for birdwatching, and there are benches and bird identification posters. They also provide an opportunity to get a view of the harbour and the cranes from a different angle. Looking in the other direction, Macedon Point juts out with a small tree planted at its tip. The original tree unfortunately died a few years ago in a hard winter, but people missed it and attempts have been made to replace it. This one seems to be surviving but it is very exposed.

This is the way you want to head on this occasion and, if the tide is out, you have the option of walking on the beach which provides a

Geese drawn by the Eel Grass exposed by the receding tide

rest for your feet. Across the lough Holywood and the green expanse of the park at Marino is usually visible with glimpses of Bangor further round the coast of County Down. Ahead, gazing past Whiteabbey the obvious white apartment blocks at Carrickfergus make it more difficult to spot the castle than it once was and the coastline is now dominated by the chimneys of the power station at Kilroot, built during the 1970s and still providing about thirty per cent of the country's electricity.

There are also paths up into Hazelbank Park so you can walk on a parallel but higher route if the mood takes you. This was once the grounds of Hazelbank House, a Georgian villa that ended up being used as Newtownabbey town hall until it was destroyed in 1972. The park has been refurbished but still keeps some of the old apple trees.

At one time handsome villas built by wealthy local mill owners existed all along the Shore Road and a few still remain. St John's Parish Church near Whitehouse was designed (like most of Belfast it seems) by Charles Lanyon who lived in the area.

At the corner where the railings join a section of stone wall look out for over-wintering Brent geese who like to feed on the eel grass growing on an outcrop of sandstone exposed when the tide is out a bit. Brents always look so neat somehow and their small size makes them easily recognisable, even to me! Every year these geese travel nearly 3000 miles from arctic Canada; usually with a short stopover in Iceland but sometimes coming straight through. They mostly go to Strangford lough before spreading out to other loughs, and there can be several dozen here at Hazelbank.

Once past the little sheltered bay which always seems to have a bit of sand above the water line you are nearly at Whiteabbey. The ruins of part of the 800 year old abbey that gave the area its name survived, up near the hospital, until a local farmer decided he needed a few stones for building in the 1920s.

You can still see the remains of an old jetty, one of two built before the channel was deepened into the port at Belfast for importing coal which was required in large quantities in this area by the numerous mills which operated here until the middle of the 20th century. Today the sad remains of the jetty is a favourite spot for cormorants in wing drying mode.

If you are still on the beach you have to come up to the road now as you have reached the point where the Three Mile Water river flows into the lough, another gathering point for gulls and oystercatchers. Sometimes there are black and white Eider ducks paddling around here too; I think they make a wonderful noise, like people having a conversation you can't quite hear.

The Old Coal Jetty

Now you can either finish here or make your way on along the coast to Jordanstown Loughshore Park. Another option, if your legs are up to it, would be to link up with the Newtownabbey Way for a longer walk, or, if you've had enough for the day, you could just stop in Whiteabbey village for some refreshments in one of the several cafes in the village.

A feast of Autumn colour going down to the river

The Newtownabbey Way

Start: Whiteabbey village
Finish: Mossley Mill, or walk back to start
How long: About 5km/3 miles one way
Type of walk: All surfaced path
Car: Parking available in Whiteabbey Village and at Mossley Mill
Public transport: Ulsterbus 163/563 or Metro 2G to start, Metro 1D to Mossley Mill.

Although you could do this walk in either direction, I usually begin from Whiteabbey village. Turning up the short road that used to go past the late Glenavna Hotel, now demolished and replaced by new housing, follow the road as it crosses the Three Mile Water River at a small bridge and becomes a pedestrian path leading up a gentle incline.

Just to the right of this path was the site of the Glen House, home of Lancelot Curran and, on a cold, dark night in November 1952, the scene of the infamous murder of his 19 year old daughter Patricia – or at least the place where her body was discovered with multiple stab wounds.

Although an airman from the local RAF station was convicted of the crime, he was cleared in 2000 when his conviction was overturned. At the time Lancelot Curran was very prominent in legal and political fields and the truth about the murder remains unresolved despite much speculation at the time and since about high level cover-ups.

An interesting contrast of styles – the original railway bridge and the later viaducts

Just part of the Bleach Green viaduct

But put thoughts of dastardly deeds behind you and continue on the path as it zigzags through a more pleasant area of large beech trees and rejoins the river just before the impressive railway viaduct where the lines north and east diverge. I especially like this part of the walk in Autumn when the leaves turn vibrant yellow and russet. As you approach the old Victorian viaduct look up and you may notice, carved on the central stone of each arch, faces that resemble the traditional Green Man, thought to be a fertility symbol – rather unusual, I would have thought, on a Victorian bridge. You then pass under the Bleach Green viaduct, named after the area where linen from the local mill was laid out to bleach in the sun. This reinforced concrete viaduct, when completed in 1933, was the longest of its type with a total length of 800 feet and reaching 70 feet in height. It is certainly impressive (apart from the graffiti, unfortunately) and if you look closely it has a slightly art deco effect decoration. I love the sweeping lines of this bridge and have even been known to bore complete strangers with information about it if they happen to be passing!

After crossing two small bridges, constructed a few years ago when this section of the Newtownabbey Way was made

"Portrait Bench" installed by Sustrans with a fisherman, a mill worker and a railway conductor chosen to represent the local community.

Alternative access path with Knockagh in the distance

more accessible, you start to come into Monkstown Wood, which is a Woodland Trust area. This wood is becoming a real haven for wildlife as the existing mature trees have been added to extensively by new planting. It has a good mix of native trees such as oak, hazel and ash, and this is great for autumn colour as well. Though you are aware that there are houses and a bus depot quite close, it really seems like an oasis away from the suburban traffic.

Once past a more open area there is an option to turn left but keep on straight following the cycle route signs for Monkstown. This section was once an extremely muddy little track known as Hurtle Toot Lane, for no reason I can discover, but it is a wonderful sounding name which is so much more evocative of Ulster than the rather bland names you see in many modern developments.

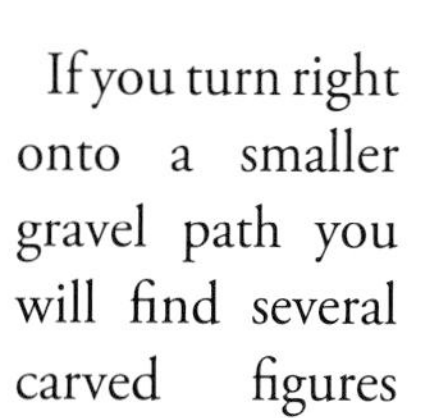

Above: The 'whale's ribcage' bridge

Right: The carving uses the natural shape of the wood

If you turn right onto a smaller gravel path you will find several carved figures made from tree trunks, using the natural shape of the wood as inspiration. This path stays with the river then joins another track which you follow to the right crossing the slightly over the top bridge resembling a whales rib cage and coming out at the cluster of shops at Monkstown crossroads. Apart from these shops the building that stands out here is Abbey Presbyterian Church; opinions are divided about the style of this but the archways along the side remind me of a Spanish hacienda which I quite like. The name Monkstown seems to be connected with an ancient, possibly even Pre-Christian, site which is at the back of an overgrown field on nearby Knockagh Road. The cemetery there was still

A carpet of larch needles softens the latest section of the path

Part of the river used to power the nearby mill

used comparatively recently, officially closing in 1958.

Cut across the car park and cross the busy road, then walk up a one way road to the left of the school. This is Bridge Road and after a short distance the way signs direct you to the right, leading into Hawthorne Road. Just above are the remains of what was known as Nellie's Dam and seemingly Bridge Road was originally called Dam Road until a local clergyman whose manse was located here objected to having this as his address.

The route continues into the Three Mile Water Park; there are some little muddy diversions through the hedgerow on the right hand side of the main path if you are in the mood for blackberries in the Autumn, but otherwise it's a straightforward path leading into the most recently opened section of the Newtownabbey Way. I was agreeably surprised when I first walked this part on a damp Autumn day; it looked as if it had been there for ages with plenty of mature larch trees dropping a carpet of orangey-brown needles on the new tarmac.

The carved trees can still be a haven to wildlife

Considerable discussion took place over how to route the new way as it approached two roads. Eventually they settled on going under the road bridge beside the river, offering an alternative route if this is flooded. You then tramp up a long wooden walkway to cross the Manse Road in the ordinary way. The final short section to Mossley Mill has information boards about the wildlife and industry of the area. Look out for the carved trees mentioned on one of the boards. These were old rotting trees which might have been in danger of falling if left to their own devices. They have been cut to a safe height and made into sculptures, so that they remain a valuable resource for insects and birds.

You have now reached Mossley Mill and can reward yourself with a cup of tea. The Mill, which is the civic centre for Newtownabbey, also boasts a museum based on the flax industry and a new theatre space. Mossley Mill itself was built in 1859 continuing a local tradition of textile manufacture. It passed through several owners who expanded both the Mill and surrounding village, using water from the river to power the spinning machinery. After it finally closed in 1995 the council took over; extending and refurbishing the existing mill buildings.

From the far side the pond looks more like a lake

The boardwalk makes a good viewing platform

After refreshments take a dander over to the Dam, a large pond where the local swans and ducks are usually looking for handouts. You can then either retrace your steps or use public transport to get back to base.

Cave hill and Collinward seen from Carnmoney hill

Carnmoney Hill

Start: Rathfern Community Activity Centre, Knockenagh Avenue
Finish: Same as start
Distance: About 3km/2 miles
Type of walk: Well marked paths but steep in places and can be muddy.
Car: Park in lay-by near entrance to Carnmoney Hill on Knockenagh Avenue
Public transport: Metro bus 2 C/D to Doagh Road

Tufted ducks on the pond

The name Carnmoney is derived from the Irish *Carn Monaidh*, meaning "cairn (or hill) of the bog" which is a bit of a clue to what you might find up there. However, the Woodland Trust has put in a number of gravelled paths in the lower areas to make this part more accessible and there are also mown grass tracks further up. I would still advise wearing boots though.

The Trust has planted up to fifty-seven thousand native trees over the hill in addition to the surviving semi-native woodland. There is ample evidence that at one time there were a surprising number of people living on the slopes of Carnmoney Hill, with old maps showing the remains of ancient raths and hidden souterrains.

This circular walk over the hill starts from the Rathfern Community Centre and play park on Knockenagh Avenue and as you go through the gate there is a Woodland Trust information board telling you a bit about their management of the woodlands.

Also near the entrance can be found a cairn on which you will find an RAF themed plaque in memory of a tragic incident during the second world war when, on St. Patrick's day 1943, a Lysander aircraft on its way to land at

Above L: The duck pond

Above R: Little bridge on the path round to Rab's

Centre: Look out for the grassy path ...

Bottom: ...leading to the track among the bluebells

Aldergrove crashed on the hill in bad weather, killing three airmen.

It is worth going over to the pond which was created when this entrance was completely revamped after being awarded funding by the People's Millions awards from the Lottery Fund in 2006. On the pond you can quite often see coots and moorhens as well as tufted duck and mallards. It's amazing how aggressive coots are for all the size of them; I once witnessed one chasing off a much larger heron from the pond when it approached the coot's young family looking for a quick snack.

Having strolled round the pond follow the markers for Rab's Pond, a small pool which was built by volunteers and has now become a bit overgrown. In the Springtime when the wild flowers are in season it is well worth taking a small diversion off the main route up a little grassy path to the right just past the pool. It leads on to a small muddy track, over a stile before veering left through a rough field and over another stile to the remains of a farm lane which takes you back on to the main path.

If you have stayed on the Rab's Pond track turn right at the end to go up the hill. On the way there is an old Victorian well just off to the left which has been restored and is worth a look though I wouldn't fancy drinking from it.

You now wind your way up through the woods. It's difficult to decide how much of this was cultivated in the past and how much is natural. A friend tells me her grandmother's house was here somewhere but she hasn't been able to identify exactly where, despite it being there in relatively recent times. I suppose it just shows how quickly nature moves back in when people move out. The trees are a mixture of ash, hazel, blackthorn and old hedgerows and under this wood anemones, violets and primroses grow happily in the spring time.

Above L: The old well made new

Above R: Following the track up hill

Centre: Through the trees in winter...

Bottom: ...or spring, each season delights in its own way

Above: From the viewpoint near the top of the hill looking towards the city and Cave hill ... or round towards Newtownabbey (below)

Blackthorn blossom

You emerge from the woods into a more open part of the route with a wonderful view over to the Cave Hill. I find this an ideal spot to pause and eat your snack (which I'm sure you had the foresight to bring) and contemplate.

If you fancy sloe gin, this is an excellent place to gather the fruit from the blackthorn bushes; there are plenty around and they really are a lovely sight in the spring when they are covered by a froth of white blossom contrasting with the dark branches.

If you wanted to do a linear variation instead of the circular route you could now go down the track to the left from here which will take you to the O'Neill Road entrance, leading past a pond on the left. There is a rath beyond the pond though it's hard to make out in the bushes.

You can turn up to the right at the long abandoned remains of farm buildings where there is a grassy path alongside an area which the Woodland Trust has planted as a wild flower meadow during the summer. A sunny day will bring out butterflies such as small tortoiseshell and orange tip fluttering between the hedgerows. Just before the path turns back down to rejoin the main track look ahead across the fields to a slight wooded hill. This is Dunanney Fort, another rath which is thought to be about 1200 years old. In the days of Elizabeth I her Lord Deputy the Earl of Sussex camped his troops around here while he met with local chieftains of the O'Neills and MacDonnells to try and come to an agreement agreeable to all parties – he was unsuccessful of course!

Going a bit further down, just before the big metal gate an old lime kiln is visible beside the track on the right. In the distant past a cart track running down from behind the Cave Hill through where Glengormley is now and down to Station Road would have been the only road existing for some distance; it became known as the Old Irish Highway and explains the concentration of activity along here.

Getting back to the circular route, from the snack stop continue on up to the right; this path gets a bit steeper here but it's worth it for the viewpoint from the log bench recently set here. There is a surprising amount of green space below amongst the housing and factories. On a clear day you can look over the city and across County Down to the distant Mourne Mountains

The grassy path can be muddy as you go a bit further up. If you walk over to the fence the summit of the hill with its trig point is visible past

The Knockagh memorial

Heading down

the TV transmitter on the left, but this is not accessible from this side. Triangulation points, the concrete pillars put up by the Ordnance Survey to help with mapping, are really redundant now we have GPS but some people are quite fond of them as landmarks and even 'collect' them by trying to visit as many as possible. It must have been some job carting the materials to make the pillars and bed them in up the hills.

Shortly after this, the path starts to descend through an open area with very young trees planted. This part is a real sea of bluebells around May time. If you look down into the valley you can make out the route of the Newtownabbey Way from the railway viaduct travelling inland along a line of trees then over to the playing fields at Threemile Water Park. Ahead of you is Knockagh Hill with its monument. This granite obelisk was put up in the 1930s but later re-dedicated in memory of the fallen of both world wars. Beyond this you can just make out Carrickfergus castle and Kilroot power station near the edge of the lough.

I wonder if this is where Lilian Bland, the first woman in Ireland and possibly anywhere to build and fly her own aeroplane, tested her prototype glider. Lilian led a varied and adventurous life for a woman of her era having had a career as a journalist and sports photographer before moving with her father to Carnmoney. In 1910 Lilian built the bi-plane glider, jokingly christened the Mayfly because it might fly or not, at her family home in Carnmoney and used the hill to try it out. She later

Take care crossing the stile

put in a 20 horse power engine which she more or less carried home on the train from England and managed to fly the plane for a short distance in trials carried out at Lord O'Neill's estate at Antrim. Lilian had thought of bringing the plane into commercial production but her interest moved on to other things when her father gave her a car on the principle that it would be less risky. She moved into car dealing for a while but was persuaded to marry a Canadian cousin and take up a comparatively quiet life farming in Vancouver. Her achievements are now commemorated with a sculpture in Glengormley park, which has also been renamed in her honour.

Another grassy stretch brings you to a gate and then between some bigger trees before going down the next section of path which requires a little care as it tends to be rather muddy. When the path forks you can go either left or right: both lead to a track between hedgerows which goes down to the right. As it bends round there is a stile which would bring you out onto a farm road leading to Ballyduff Brae; but for this walk you want to keep on the track and follow it as it meanders downhill to a metal gate type stile and onto a concrete road.

This is Fernlea Lane and it brings you out onto the Doagh Road. Walk a short distance to the right and turn right again up a paved footpath beside some houses; a short cut through to a car park. Just beyond the grassy slope in front of you is the play park where you began the walk.

Belfast Castle

Belfast Castle and Lower Cave Hill

START: BELFAST CASTLE CAR PARK ACCESSED FROM INNISFAYLE PARK
FINISH: SAME AS START
DISTANCE: ABOUT 4KM/2.5 MILES
TYPE OF WALK: MOSTLY GRAVEL PATH BUT ONE STEEP OFF PATH SECTION WHICH CAN BE MUDDY.
CAR: BELFAST CASTLE CAR PARK
PUBLIC TRANSPORT: METRO BUS 1B/C/D TO ANTRIM ROAD

Above: The formal Cat Garden with its hidden cats … although (right) this one's easy to find

The car park at the castle, accessed via Innisfayle Park, is the start point for this walk which takes you up the hill to just below the caves. Begin by going through the barrier and past the castle itself. On the way you could stroll round the formal Cat Garden to see if you can find the nine cats represented in various ways. There is a story that the presence of a cat, preferably white, at the castle will ensure good luck to the inhabitants.

Designed by Lanyon in the Scottish baronial style for George Chichester, the third Marquis of Donegall, whose coat of arms appears above the front door, I can only assume no cats were present during the building of the castle for it ran far over the original budget of £11,000.

This was a major problem for the family as the Marquis' father, the second Marquis had gambled away most of his inheritance. He had served as Lord Lieutenant of Donegal despite a session in debtor's prison which he escaped by marrying into the May family (who themselves had a far from pristine reputation but at least had the money to allow him to buy his way out of prison) and who accompanied him later when he came to live at the estate in Ormeau to escape his creditors in England earning him the nickname of 'Lord Done-'em-all'. More extravagance led to the marquis having to sell off leases for the family's holdings in large parts of Belfast, more or less ending the influence, dating back to the 1600s, of the Chichester family in the city. Their work in developing Belfast is still evident in the various streets named after them, and the Mays also are remembered in place names such as Maysfield, whether they deserve it or not.

The castle was only completed when the third Marquis' son-in-law Lord Ashley, later Earl of Shaftsbury stepped in to finance its completion. The impressive outside staircase round the other side so popular with wedding photographers was added later by the ninth earl for his mother's birthday. Quite a present! The castle was eventually presented to the city. More recently it closed for a major restoration reopening in 1988, and now has an interesting display upstairs about its history and the wildlife on the hill. You can also have some refreshments down in the cellars; they are quite tolerant of soggy walkers in the café!

But back to the walk. At the right-hand side of the next big gate there is a pedestrian entrance so go through this. There is another car park here accessed from the Antrim Road but you should turn up a track to the left by the information board and stay with it as it swings right keeping straight on

The Volunteer's Well

past a couple of paths on the left. When you meet another path coming up from the driveway for the second car park, turn left up the hill with a stream on your right.

The going gets a bit harder now so I like to stop for a rest when I reach the Volunteer's Well. Apparently this spot was a popular meeting place for picnickers in the past as well as those en route for the fairs held further up the hill in days gone by, although I'm not sure if the name refers to the stream or the little round stone structure, now filled in. This seems more decorative than useful, being so near the actual stream. The tradition of the well being used by volunteers who trained on the hill in the late eighteenth century was part of the evidence used to show that the path was a public right of way, when it was blocked in the 1850s by merchant Joseph Magill building part of his grandiose Martlett Towers estate over it. A court case was brought against him by local people with help from the Association for the Protection of Rights of Way, which Martlett lost. His claims that the path was only used by respectable acquaintances he approved of held no water when one witness revealed his wife made a business out of selling poteen to anyone passing. Others said the path was used by peat cutters and to get to the fairs up near the caves, part of a bridle way from the shore to Glenavy beginning at Gray's Lane. The case was very high profile with local newspaper The Northern Whig publishing the whole transcript of the trial in a booklet. Paying the costs of the case led to Magill becoming bankrupt. The land went to the castle estate with the house being used for workers, and the right of way was kept open although part it was moved over a bit.

A blue arrow here tries to send you to the left but I prefer the rather more adventurous route carved by mountain bikes ahead to the right up a kind of muddy groove. This means you have the opportunity to admire the impressive mature beech trees whose pale bark is especially eye-catching when the branches are bare in winter. Climbing up through these trees is pretty steep and you may have to clamber over the odd fallen tree, but follow the stone stumps of what seems to be an old wall, which can be used as steps. The ground

Winter Beech Trees

begins to level as you find yourself in a hollow among the trees which usually has a huge puddle in the middle. Skirt round this and carry on passing some old concrete fence posts lying to your right, part of an old boundary fence. There is a gap between sawn logs where a tree has fallen and been cut through and then head for a break in the trees bringing you come out onto the civilised gravel path.

Nearly all the climbing is over now as you walk left along this path below the looming cliffs. Other little paths lead up to the lower cave and on up the hill but for now stay on the main one. The five caves themselves seem to be a bit of a mystery, they are probably at least partly man-

Looking up to the caves

made but nobody is sure of their age or what they were used for though there are suggestions that they may have been connected with ancient mining for iron ore. Below the caves is a large hollow known as the Devil's Punchbowl, which was probably an early quarry. The story goes that cattle were kept in this area when the traditional fairs, whose existence was one of the reasons the right of way case was successful, took place up here.

A recent addition to the left of the path are several carved stone stools designed by local school children – a good spot to perch and admire the view out over the city before heading back down through the woods. After a steepish bit of path rutted by tree roots and a couple of sets of deep steps the route stays at a fairly even height along the side of the hill above the castle – glimpsed through the trees it looks like something out of a fairy story. The Marquis had the castle built in his existing deer park, and at that stage trees had been cleared and the ground was much more open. Further planting has since joined up with the remaining hazel woods to so that if you look up from the lough shore the castle seems to be growing out of the forest.

The slopes on the right above as you continue on can be lovely when strewn with bluebells or willow herb, and in the winter watch out for an amazing tree which kept on growing after collapsing completely to the ground, more visible when the leaves are off. In amongst the trees and

Bluebells in the woods

The tree that wouldn't give up

Fairy tale view of Belfast Castle

shrubs above, a few bricks are all that remains of the game keeper's cottage, unoccupied when it burned down in 1957. It's difficult to believe that people lived up there within living memory; like the house of my friend's grandmother on Carnmoney Hill, nature has quickly re-asserted herself and taken over!

It never fails to amaze me how quickly, if left to her own devices, nature will move in to cover up the scars we make on the landscape. Another example of this can be found nearby where, during a raid in WWII, a German bomb exploded near the castle making a large crater which is barely visible today unless you search it out.

More well known is the tragic crash of an American B-17 fighter plane on its way to Nutt's Corner airport. The plane dropped too low in heavy fog and struck the side of the hill, killing all on board. The story of the fairly recent discovery of a crew member's ring near the sight of the crash and the tracking down of the owner's widow was romanticised in Richard Attenborough's film *Closing the Ring*.

Another story about the hill was revived a few years ago with the rediscovery of the Cave Hill 'diamond'. This fist-sized lump of translucent quartz was originally found by a small boy somewhere on the hill and bought by a Belfast shopkeeper who made quite a thing of it and put it on show in his window. It was rumoured to have been sold to Madame Tussaud's, but was recently found by a descendant of the shopkeeper and given to the Linenhall Library. How it got onto the Cave Hill is a puzzle, as this type of quartz doesn't naturally occur here.

You could now take a shortcut back down to the castle by following one of the gravel tracks on the left, otherwise stay with the one you are on until it too swings left and joins the track coming in from the Upper Cavehill Road. Turn left and you arrive at the driveway to the car park, but if you go right towards the gates a slight detour down Innisfayle Park will give you the chance to glimpse the Marquis of Donegall's old church and family vault, the Chapel of the Resurrection. The third Marquis had the chapel built by the firm of Lanyon and Lynn, but after about fifty years it fell into disuse and was eventually handed over to the council who in turn gave it to the Church of Ireland. After years of vandalism and neglect it was de-consecrated and sold to a building firm then sold on again. Houses have grown up around it so you have to peek along one of the driveways to see it from the road. Hopefully the chapel's current owners and those campaigning on its behalf will be successful in finding a way this handsome building can be restored and used by the community.

Returning to the Castle gates pick up the footpath again so you can make your way back to your starting point from a different angle with a good view up to the castle.

View from near McArts Fort

Cave Hill and Ballyaghagan

Start: Belfast Zoo car park off the Antrim Road
Finish: Same as start
Distance: About 8km/5 miles
Type of walk: Some quite rough tracks, steep sections and open moorland, boots advised.
Car: Park in Belfast Zoo Carpark
Public transport: Metro bus 1 B/C/D stop near Zoo

This is a longer and a bit more adventurous walk than the Lower Cave Hill one although it can still be completed in about three hours. The start is the car park at Belfast Zoo and from there you follow the track round to the right of the zoo wall at the two information boards. Climb up the stone steps into the hazel woods, turning right at the top, up a few more steps and along a rough path with sort of big stone cobbles, mostly covered with soil now. The path becomes muddier as it winds upwards, passing an oddly placed (there's no view!) carved wooden bench as it bends left. There has been a fair bit of work done here to clear invasive tree species leaving more room for the old long established hazels which, in the past, local people may have coppiced to provide fencing and firewood. There are plenty of wildflowers scattered through the woods; in the spring watch out especially for bluebells, delicate white wood anemones, primroses, ramsons, with their strong garlicky smell, and

Spring bluebells by the path

lesser celandine. Later in the year you often find nuts from the hazels on the path, dropped by the squirrels – grey ones unfortunately – or birds.

It's best to watch your step as you carry on past a slope with evergreen trees growing as there are some holes on the right of the path which used to be badger setts.. The path continues zigzagging uphill, climbing some more

Belfast lough glimpsed through the trees

Ballyaghagan cairn – not much is visible

steps and passing another bench before joining a narrower track where you turn left. You are starting to get into more open terrain here, and after getting across a stream (usually no problem unless there has been torrential rain recently) you come out onto open hillside which is a good place to pause, get your breath and take in the view over to Belfast Lough and Knockagh hill.

The grassy path is still easy to follow and has been stabilised in places with wooden planks making steps. After a mini cattle grid and another little stream a more obvious track has been made with a gravel surface. As you continue onward look out for a stile over the fence to the right. This takes you off the gravel track onto a little trodden path which goes up more or less beside the fence until it reaches a grassy bump with some stones on top.

Now is the time for a small celebration because you are on the summit of the hill, Ballyaghagan cairn. The cairn, which may date from Neolithic times, looks more like a hole in the ground than a cairn but apparently that's because most of it has been covered by peat over the years.

Your reward for the climb is a 360 degree panorama of the province. Off to the left there is McArt's Fort which sits out so prominently that most people head for it and think it's the top; however the cairn is a few metres higher up and we'll save the fort for the return part of the walk.

View to the distant Mourne Mountains

Hawthorn berries give a splash of colour in the autumn

Squire's hill

There are several theories about why it's called McArt's Fort. It has been suggested it was after Art O'Neill the 16th century chieftain, or perhaps from from a legendary hero descended from the ninth century king who gave the area its previous name of Ben Madigan. That is unless Ben Madigan is taken from the Irish meaning 'hill of the red dog'. Take your pick! The fort itself is probably iron-age and so would predate Art but perhaps he used it later bequeathing it his name. Certainly the O'Neills were powerful in the area and legend tells of the existence of a natural 'throne' in the rocks on top of the fort being used for coronations by the clan. Today no evidence of the throne remains at the fort as, following a newspaper story about it in a nationalist

The Cashel

newspaper, in the 1890s it was prized from the ground and sent over the edge of the cliff by those disapproving of such things. Despite its destruction, its memory lives on in the area of the city known as the Throne which lies in the shadow of the hill.

Looking north along the coast on a clear day you can make out in the far distance the Antrim Hills, then going anticlockwise the characteristic cone shape of Slemish, Lough Neagh, the rest of the Belfast Hills, further off Slieve Croob and the Mourne Mountains, Scrabo Tower and Strangford Lough and back to Belfast. On a calm summer's day I love to perch on a stone and hear the skylarks singing as they do their vertical takeoff act. I expect it's territorial and, to skylarks, quite threatening but I find listening to it very therapeutic.

Backtrack a couple of metres and pick out the narrow squelchy path over the heath heading away from McArt's, cutting through the heather roughly west along the ridge of the hill (another path heads over towards Collinward Hill, with a mast a bit like a pylon on top so take care to pick the one to the left of this). This upland area feels very different from the woods and grassy bits lower down, with the classic heath mix of heathers, bilberries and sphagnum moss, although unfortunately it has suffered from the effects of wildfires over the years. The hill with the mast on ahead of you in the distance is Squire's Hill, with Divis and Black's Mountain behind and to the south of it.

Somewhere amongst these hills is reputed to rest the hidden loot of highwayman Naose O'Haughan and his robber band, undiscovered since his execution near Carrickfergus in 1720. Naoise was the last of three brothers to be captured, probably due to his ability to leap vast distances, according to legend anyway. This amazing athletic skill is an oft recurring theme in legends of Irish outlaws and there seems to have been leaping rapparees all over the country.

The wee path comes to a mossy knoll and skirts along the side of the hill then swings down to the right. Looking round now you have in view to the right the old quarry and landfill site. This is coming to the end of its use but I met a young woman here on one occasion whose job involved checking the upright pipes bedded down into various parts of the landfill to monitor methane levels. Apparently the levels were satisfactorily low but are only one of the things which will still need to be monitored when the lorries which can still be seen trundling around in there are long gone. Recent waste buried seems to have been sort of shrink wrapped, which means they can't plant trees or the roots might damage the bundles. I wonder if they just left the whole thing to its own devices, how quickly nature would take over. Unfortunately we haven't seen the last of the rubbish trucks up here as the company are now opening up the old quarry on the right for use as a waste management area.

Snow softens the gravel track

Gradually you come down again to long grass. Meander down the hill until you have forded a small stream then swing left round some bushes to a stile, watching out for a bit of a ditch just before you reach it. This gives a way through an area of gorse and scrub mixed into overgrown hedgerows; great for wildlife. A friend spotted a long eared owl here in an aged thorn tree one morning but of course I missed it!

After crossing the stile, walk a few metres then climb diagonally through the thorn trees on your right looking out for the back of an old rusty sign which will help you to find another stile in the fence a little to the right of it. A short bumpy path through a break amongst whin bushes gets you onto a stony track. Going this way avoids a very marshy section where I think there must be a stream under the turf.

When you see a bank constructed on the left of the track climb on to it and go along the top. Scan the field on the other side of this bank and you will be able to make out the raised circular outline of a large cashel, or stone ring fort. Carefully climb over the sort of D-I-Y stile near the far end and look across the field for the next stile near the Hightown Road car park. Sometimes there are cattle grazing in here, so you should use discretion, especially if there are calves among them.

Milewater waterfall

The cashel was the scene not long ago of an archaeological dig by a team from Queen's in association with the council and the Belfast Hill's Partnership. It was pretty wet and cold over the weeks when the dig took place, but there was a fair bit of enthusiasm from local schools and the public who were encouraged to get involved. Results indicated that there was occupation in the Neolithic period followed by the early medieval cashel, which looks to have been more to show off than to keep enemies out, and a later farmhouse built straddling the cashel in the 1600s.

Cut over to another stile to reach the surfaced track leading from the car park and follow this keeping to the right when it forks near a miniature waterfall. This is the Mile Water appearing before heading under the path and down Carr's Glen and amazingly this used to be the main water supply when Belfast was a much smaller town. Several mills grew up alongside this little river, which lower

Well worn path to McArt's fort

down feeds into the reservoirs at the Waterworks park.

The left fork would take you back up to the top but that's too easy! So keep on the downward track for a bit longer until an awkwardly built stile into a field appears on your left. Once over a gentle diagonal climb through the lush grass brings you to a gap in the hedgerow where another surfaced path emerges. Keep on up through the gap with the old limestone quarry to your right. This was in use in the nineteenth century, with the limestone being transported down by rail along the Cavehill and Limestone Roads to the docks. This path goes up to join the main track but a little informal one turns right at the new viewpoint cairn and passes along the top edge of the quarry then wends its way up the side of the hill. This can be soft underfoot especially if mountain bikes have been down it recently so watch your footing as you head back up towards McArt's fort. Another great view of the city unfolds as you climb; everything seems to sparkle, especially when the sun comes out after the rain.

You can head over a little causeway bridging the ditch and straight up some steps onto the fort from this side and pause to take in the sights once more. Bear in mind you are at the top of a cliff here; so if you want to look out for the resident ravens wait till you are further down. Tradition has it that

Pause to enjoy the sweeping views of the city

leading members of the United Irishmen including Wolfe Tone and Henry Joy McCracken came up the hill to meet and it was here they swore the oath that moved them from working for equal rights to open rebellion, inspired by the revolutions in France and America. Members of the group later hid out in the hills round Belfast and McCracken was indeed captured on the Cave Hill.

Heading down some different plank edged steps opposite the cliff edge brings you back onto the main path, so turn right here and descend to the gravelly bit you met when coming up. After the mini cattle grid you could just retrace your steps down to the zoo, but for variety I like to swing down to the right on the path that clings to the hill below the famous caves. From here you can look up the steep rocky cliff with McArt's perched on top and check for the kestrel's nest somewhere high on the inaccessible crags.

Carry on along the path and round to the left descending into the woods once more. Strange animal cries may reach you but hopefully they are coming from inside the zoo as this path wanders along the strong boundary fence. It dips past the rear of the tiger enclosure and up again eventually bringing you back to the top of the stone steps and back to the zoo car park.

Subtle colours mark the seasons on the way up to Divis

Divis Summit

Start: National Trust car park on Divis Rd.
Finish: Same as start
How long: About 6.5km/4 miles
Type of walk: Up hill but on good tracks and surfaced road
Car: Park at NTcar park on Divis Rd. off Upper Springfield Road
Public transport: Ulsterbus 106 to Crumlin via Hannahstown, but stops a mile from the start.

The Long Barn

This walk mostly makes use of the recently constructed summit trail onto the top of Divis; it makes a nice contrast to the much squishier Divis Circuit walk although both have their charms. The name Divis means black ridge, hopefully not referring to the weather as the hill itself seems quite green from this angle. The high point of the hill is 478 metres above sea level but you only have to climb about 180 of them if you start from the National Trust car park. This is quite a popular area for dog walkers as you can just walk up to the mast and down on the surfaced road. Hopefully you will take my advice and venture on to a slightly more interesting route, though you get brilliant views and wide open spaces whichever way you go.

From the car park walk up the tarmac drive to the Long Barn Visitor Centre. It was once a farm building but has been converted by the National Trust and has toilets and an information point if open. There is also an area for picnics and a pleasant pond and another car park is under development. Recently an archaeological dig took place behind the barn in an area destined to become a car park. Like the one at Ballyaghagan this was organised by the Belfast Hills Partnership and involved public participation, though I don't think they found anything particularly dramatic on this occasion. People seem to really enjoy getting

Old thorn trees

their hands dirty and taking part in these things even if the results are not very spectacular. A number of worked flints and some possibly medieval pottery fragments were discovered, and a rectangle of stones which look like they were laid down as the floor of a mud built cottage.

Take the gravelled path opposite, on the left through the gate. The path swings right bringing you above the site of an ancient settlement, visible as a vague circle of stones in the grass. Nearby on the hill there is also an unusual double walled enclosure of a kind more commonly found in Scotland illustrating the close links that have existed between Ulster and Scotland down through time.

In the past it was believed that the fairies were responsible for these rings; so you had to be careful not to mess with them or your cow's milk would dry up or worse. To counteract such malevolent forces, folklore provided various remedies including one concoction using flint arrowheads which people attributed to the fairies as well. Such arrowheads can be found widely in the Divis area and indeed there are so many ancient remains scattered about up here that I often wonder which of the lumps and bumps might turn out to be twelve thousand year old settlements, medieval farmhouses – or just bumps!

On the path here is a large information board showing

Ponds near the barn

a time-line of historical milestones. I like to pause here sometimes and try to imagine how things were around a thousand years ago when the early farmers built the rath. They probably chose to live up on the hillside because the lower ground would have been covered by dense woodland, where wolves and wild boar roamed.

Just after this the left hand path joins the new trail, which zigzags its way up to the mast at the top, via several bits of stone wall which I think are meant to act as seats so you can perch and contemplate. The buildings and mast were originally erected by the Ministry of Defence in the cold war period and then, due to their commanding views of the city, were used as an observation base during the Troubles. The buildings are now unmanned. When the army moved on the National Trust managed to buy the surrounding land, and they found that nature had actually benefitted from the lack of disturbance by the public while the army was there. The

It's a gentle climb to the summit

various masts up here are not terribly picturesque but they do make useful navigation aids and, through long association, seem almost part of the hill.

The view from up here is wonderful so try to choose a clear day to get the benefit of this panorama across to Lough Neagh and the Sperrins, or over to Donegal. Mind you, you can start out on a clear day and move through several different climates before the end of your walk. Still, you can always shelter from the wind behind the MoD buildings so that's another use for them even if they aren't very pretty.

By the way, there seem to be a couple of laws of nature that affect this hill as I've found to my cost;

The rolling countryside looking over to Lough Neagh

Number one – if a friend who has never been up says they would like to go up Divis and you offer to escort them there and tell them how brilliant the views are, no matter how fine the weather is elsewhere when you go there will be a cloud stuck on the top and;

Number two – if you bring a clean dog with you, you stick to the track and the weather is dry, it is a certainty that the clean dog will still find something disgusting to roll in!

The top of the mountain was where first use was made of the Drummond Light during the ordnance survey mapping of Ireland in 1828. This device, invented by Captain Thomas Drummond based on the principles of lime light, emitted an extremely bright light which could be seen at great distances making it possible to take trigonometric measurements between widely separated trig points, helping to make mapping more accurate. The

The new path makes things easier

Croob and the Mournes. Sometimes being on an even surface like this can have advantages – it means you don't have to watch your feet all the time so you can look around you. Once past the TV mast, a familiar landmark since 1955 when it was the first permanent transmitter in Ireland, why not take a detour left up the boardwalk and along the new track over to the top of Black Mountain for even more spectacular views.

a visitor – were killed with an axe and his house set alight, presumably to try and cover up the crime. No solution was ever found to the case.

The new ridge trail continues on (see Divis Circuit walk) for a longer walk but to return you can just reverse back to the main track and it's an easy stroll straight down past the Barn to the entrance.

light from this instrument when set up on on Divis was visible on Slieve Snaght in Donegal some 68 miles away.

Drummond later moved into politics and was appointed Irish Under Secretary in Dublin heading up the administration in Dublin Castle.

After going past the mast join the tarmac track which swings right to go down the hill. Now you get sweeping views over the city to Strangford Lough and further afield to Slieve

On the other side of Black Mountain is the mysterious Hatchet Field, its odd shape distinctive because the grassy vegetation differs in colour from its surroundings. Strangely a hatchet was involved in some grisly murders that took place at this spot in the 1750s. Three people – cattle drover William Cole, his daughter and

You can enjoy the view going down the track

Belfast Lough comes into view

Divis Circuit

Start: NT car park on Divis Rd.
Finish: Same as start
How long: About 11km/7 miles
Type of walk: Rough and boggy ground, some up hill, boots essential
Car: Park at National Trust car park on Divis Rd. off Upper Springfield Road
Public transport: Ulsterbus 106 to Crumlin via Hannahstown, but stops mile from start.

Sun and shadow over Divis

This is definitely a boot walk and not one for anybody who minds getting a bit muddy; indeed, unless you're really into getting covered in wet mud it would be best done in the summer or after a good dry spell!

Starting from the National Trust car park cross the road to the entrance gate and clamber over a wooden stile beside the gate on your left. You are immediately on very squelchy bog but can negotiate with care over to firmer ground near the fence alongside the road. Once on dry land you can pause to appreciate the flora of the bog – the fluffy white seed heads of Bog Cotton, the little yellow star like flowers of Bog Asphodel and if you look closely you might spot carnivorous fly-catching Sundews low down on the surface.

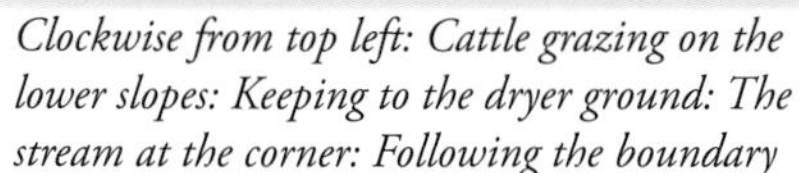

Clockwise from top left: Cattle grazing on the lower slopes: Keeping to the dryer ground: The stream at the corner: Following the boundary

Keep going parallel to the fence through an area that used to be a military firing range; you can see a building that they used for storage up to the right.

As you walk along you get glimpses of the past when small farms were scattered over the hills. Here and there the ridges left by lazy beds are visible in the turf and bits of old track marked by thorn trees. Sheep farming was once the mainstay of agriculture here, but now, apart from the occasional horse, there are only cattle. The way they graze, not cropping too short, is better for the development of the natural plant life such as heathers although their greater weight can do more damage to the ground.. The grassy areas are interspersed with wetter ground known as flushes with little springs running through, where bog plants and rushes flourish.

Near the corner of the fence there is a stream where the ground is churned up by the cattle and you may have to make use of bits of fallen trees to get across. Further on another stream appears, the early stages of the Crumlin River marked impressively on the map as the Head of the Waters, but it's an easier crossing than the previous one as there's more rocks to step on. If you can tell where the animals have crossed follow the footprints as they generally know the best place to get over.

Five rivers have their birth on round Divis, – the Colin, Forth and Ballygomartin as well as the Crumlin and Clady Water. Water from these rivers used to power the mills and supply the population of Belfast until it grew too large to be sustained by this means. Water was then piped from the Mourne Mountains to the city.

As you walk up to the right you are leaving the road behind and getting into wilder countryside but you still have the boundary fence to guide you. There is a large crater on the left, probably made when obtaining stones for farm buildings, then a couple of ridges made by the remains of low walls – part of the old famine wall built on the city boundary to give employment to the poor. In those days it wasn't considered right to give people money unless they were doing some form of labour; mustn't spoil them after all! Following on up the side of Armstrong's Hill the fence turns left but you can keep out a bit from it as long as visibility is good to avoid the worst of the marshy, rushy parts and cut the corners.

Another little river, the Clady Water, comes down here; unless you want to experience a sinking feeling beware the brown earthy bits on the banks as you cross and try to keep to bits with grass on. This should be a good area for snipe as apparently they like soft ground because it's easier to get worms and insects. Red grouse can be found around here where there are new heather shoots and there may also be the odd Irish Hare up on Divis, but they are difficult to spot especially as they can run at up to thirty miles an hour so will be well out of the way if they see you coming.

Around this area is the townland of Altigarron, meaning small hill of the horses (so they must have been up here a long time!) where a number of families are known to have lived in the early twentieth century. With the fence still off to your left go straight up past a small concrete structure and through a heathery patch that is lovely in late summer. When you hit the fence again follow it to the right; you will still need to circle out from the fence to keep out of the worst of

Which way now? Follow the post

the wet ground. Glance over to your left here to get a good view of Squire's Hill and Cave Hill. The fence soon bends left but keep going straight to avoid another boggy area downhill on the left where some more streams begin.

A slight indication of a track and buried walls running straight ahead (another bit of the famine wall) should be discernible; becoming more obvious with a few tattered thorn trees beside it. Look out for a cluster of posts of various kinds, a couple of metal ones and wooden markers that seem to have lost their

Standing stone

direction arrows. This means you have connected with part of the old shorter marked walk that comes round Divis so follow it up to the left. There is a the trodden path and markers along the route, but there are also a few wee streams and more marshy bits to cross though some have planks as improvised bridges.

Coming onto the surfaced lane follow it right keeping an eye out for the standing stone just on the other side of the fence to the left on Mount Gilbert. This is a great viewpoint to look out over the hills, lough and city, directly facing the famous cranes. To the north is Wolf Hill, where legend has it that the last wolf in Ulster was

Coming round the mountain ...the effort was worth it!

killed in the 1700s. Although wolves had been on the decline since the Cromwellian war in Ireland in the mid 1600s when generous bounties were offered for killing them, I'm not sure how they would have known it was the last one at the time!

If you are really determined you can keep with the boundary fence but this is again pretty boggy so the newly established Ridge Trail makes a tempting alternative. Once past the masts down on your left a boardwalk leads across the soggy ground then its onto a gravel track up past the boulder, carried here in the ice age, known as the Bobby Stone – a well known local

The Bobby Stone

Trig point on Black mountain

landmark as you approach the top of the Mountain. On old maps it's marked as the Babbystone or Baby Stone so it's uncertain where the name originates. For unknown reasons somebody seems to have attempted to blow it up at some stage; maybe it was the army using it for target practice.

A trig point marks the top with brilliant views of the city below with the two yellow cranes a dominant feature. You can dip down to the fence line to get a closer look. I don't know why it is so fascinating to try and spot familiar landmarks in the city spread out below but everybody seems to do it. Walking along here I've often I got the feeling I was being followed by the Tesco store on the Ballygomartin Road, it is always in view! Below are the limestone quarries which gave the Whiterock area its name.

Having followed the track down the other side of Black Mountain you come to a fence but there is a stile beside the gate. Here again you now have a choice, keep with the Ridge Trail or go straight ahead. If taking the straight ahead option the ground is rather soft again in the valley so it's a good idea to keep along the slightly higher ground near the line of poles at the left. Before getting to Black Hill veer right past the remains of walls and foundations where the old gamekeeper's cottage used to be. The cottage

Dry path at last

Remains of gamekeeper's cottage

was occupied by one of the gamekeepers employed by landowner Lord Templeton of Templepatrick, the other one living in Divis Lodge over beside the Long Barn. The way is straight on keeping more or less the same height until you arrive at a wire fence, hopefully near a small three barred stile which you climb over. Now head down to the river looking out for a man-made ridge structure, one of two dams connected with McCance's Mill below in the Collin valley. Near this point the river narrows enough to step over easily, then it's a question of keeping well above the fence on your left and working through more rushy terrain. Just above the Long Barn is a bit of boardwalk to carry you over the last extra boggy ditch, so try and aim for that.

However you may well feel you have had enough bog for one day and the new Ridge Trail offers the dry feet option as it takes a winding route, contouring round the hill. They have done a great job with this trail, using gravel interspersed with attractive stone slabs over wet sections.

Crossing a new stile and heading back via a small bridge it hits the access road just above the barn and once on the tarmac road simply stroll back down to the car park.

Nearly back to the Barn

The Glen – a green oasis

Colin Glen

Start: Colin Glen car park off Stewartstown Road
Finish: Same as start
How long: About 6.5km/4 miles
Type of walk: All surfaced path except for round pond
Car: Colin Glen Car Park
Public transport: Metro bus 10B/F

The car park for Colin Glen is on the Stewartstown Road and this is where you begin the walk.

There seems to be some disagreement over whether the name has one L or two, maybe because the word comes not from someone's name but from the Irish for high ground, presumably describing Colin Hill. There is also another suggestion that Colin comes from the word for Holly.

A huge information board up in front of the café tells highlights from the history and folklore of the glen. In recent history the lower glen lost a lot of its trees during the world wars when many oaks were felled to assist in the war effort which, in conjunction with more being taken for use in the furniture industry, seriously depleted the forest.

Luckily further destruction of the woods was halted when, in 1945, the National Trust appealed for funds for the purchase of the upper glen. The subscriptions reached the target a couple of years later and the Glen became one of the Trust's first properties in Northern Ireland. Although the new owner prevented further depletion of trees over time the glen suffered from serious neglect and I believe it was a terrible mess until the mid 80s when volunteers and local school children joined in an enormous clean up and replanting of

Early purple Orchid

native trees such as oak, hazel and willow.

But enough of history and time to enjoy the results of all these efforts. Once through the big gate at the end of the car park the footpath heads along the right-hand side of the river. Straight away you are in a leafy oasis speckled with white anemones and ramsons in their season. Spring is the best time to see wild flowers when the emerging new leaves on the trees still allow enough light to filter through. Keep to the left hand path at each of the three forks, gradually working your way up until reaching another left turn to circle the wildlife lake. The first time I went this way with a friend we were really disappointed when we saw the little pond you come to on the right. My friend and I walked round it spotting tadpoles and saying to ourselves that calling it a lake was a bit of an exaggeration, then we realised there were boys fishing just around the corner and we were not at the actual lake at all.

The area round here was reclaimed after it was used for landfill on the closure of the brickworks operation that took place here up to the 1960s. You can take a dander round

The wildlife pond

the perimeter to check for wildfowl until nearly back where you started at the outlet. Cross the little bridge then take the trodden dirt path to the left which leads you back to the track you were on before this detour. Continue left past a couple of other turn offs then down to the right to the Tri-Bridge with its three 'legs' (one of several constructed during the clean up) which crosses over to the other side of the river. Follow it up stream where it dives under the Glen Road and you will see two muddy paths.

One climbs up quite steeply to a path along the edge of the glen. This would take you through the upper glen and Glenside Community Wood past an old quarry and can be used to for a link walk to Divis, by crossing the road and going up towards the mast on Black's Hill.

However, on this occasion opt for the left hand route for a bit of an explore through another pleasant woodland coming to the end of the path at the remains of an extinct bridge. The river has formed a ravine here, with layers of rock in the cliff known as the Colin Glen Fault which is of great interest to geologists. Apparently all the different types of rock laid down in the Belfast area over a period of 160 million years are exposed here but you would need to be an expert to spot them. They say fossils are quite common on the river bed, though collectors have been coming here since Victorian times so there may not be any left by now! Colin Glen was one of the first locations to inspire the newly formed amateur natural history and geology societies that emerged during the nineteenth century, such as the Belfast Naturalists Society, who were particularly impressed by the ferns growing on the banks. Fern collecting was very fashionable at the time and I'm always amazed at how adventurous and keen Victorian women were as naturalists – it must have been hard going trekking up rivers and climbing hills in those voluminous long skirts, all in aid of finding a new specimen.

As you look up the river it's easy to believe that this was a place where wolves prowled until the seventeenth century and people felt close to the supernatural. The story goes that

Steps to the upper glen

In the Ravine

a local man by the name of Den McGaw had an encounter with a mysterious black bull which blocked his way when he was trying to cross the river. Each time he moved along the bank to try and get over, the bull on the other bank moved also. At last Den threw his knife at the bull, but it just glanced off its skin and caused the animal to charge across the water at him, whereupon Den fled back home and slammed the door. The story must be true, they say, because the bull's footprints can be seen on a big stone in the river. And I'm sure if you look hard enough, you'll find them!

This was a sort of optional extra to the walk as now you simply retrace your steps back under the Glen Road and on down the river, this time staying on its left hand bank. This side is just as attractive as the other, alive with birdsong and the gentle purling of the water. It feels so timeless it's difficult to believe the glen was in such a bad way only twenty years or so ago. I haven't been here in the Autumn yet, but I think it would be pretty spectacular with all the deciduous trees changing colour. Probably be great for fungi on the forest floor too, so that is definitely going in the diary.

After passing the Tri-Bridge again the next one you see is the Weir Bridge marking where the mill race was constructed that turned the wheel of the McCance's linen mill on the Suffolk Road. The McCance family were influential in the

The Weir Bridge

Strolling down the glen

Gamekeeper's bridge

area for nearly two hundred years until the 1920s and the gradual decline of the linen industry. The glen was also used as an amenity and for shooting game. Further on there is another bridge known as the Gamekeeper's Bridge after the original toll bridge where the gamekeeper reputedly charged for crossing over to Hannahstown. Today you get to cross free of charge then a left turn and you are back on the first section of track back to the car park.

The sound of the river keeps you company as you go

Winter magic – the Lagan from Ormeau Bridge

Dunmurry to Yorkgate Station with Giant's Ring Loop

Start: Dunmurry railway station
Finish: Yorkgate station
How long: About 19km/12 miles
Type of walk: Surfaced paths and quiet roads except Giant's Ring
Car: Park at Dunmurry station then train back
Public transport: Portadown train to Dunmurry, Larne line to Yorkgate

Glen River

This is another walk that works well using the train; if you get off at Dunmurry station walk left down into the village and turn right onto Kingsway to reach the Jubilee Park on the left. The path beside the pleasant little Glen river does a sort of U-turn just before houses and goes up steps to some playing fields. In the days when this area was largely agricultural the grain produced was ground for flour at a mill powered by this small burn, which appears to be a continuation of the Colin river; later on they used steam power.

Cut across to the right round the edge of the playing fields to come out beside a play park onto the Glenburn Road. They have very inconsiderately put the M1 here so you need to go left then right onto Dunmurry Lane to cross over the motorway and keep on until you see a wooden gate on the right giving access to a small gravel track through some woods.

At first the track seems to be heading back to the motorway but it swings left up hill near a fence. When you come to a T-junction veer right to reach the River Lagan now visible ahead. The path follows downstream along the edge of Sir Thomas and Lady Dixon Park, unless you want to digress to have a look round the delightful rose garden.

Heading into Dixon's Park

Originally a farming estate the park passed through various hands before being given to the city by Lady Dixon as a memorial to her husband. American troops were stationed at the estate in WWII and Lady Dixon was made a Dame in honour of her assistance at that time.

The tranquil Lagan

Keep with the river as much as you can and don't worry when you have to detour a bit round an unfortunate enclosure with rubbish skips. You can soon head down some steps and over a foot bridge to reach the Drum Bridge; having made your way under this look out for a bollard on your right, the only visible remnant of the sixth lock on the canal (coming from Belfast) apart from the original lock house which still stands here in the park, but is private.

The route carries on past a sign which says 5 miles to Stranmillis, with the river still on your right. The tow path here follows the disused canal and the fallen trees and overgrown water plants make it a sheltered refuge for wildlife. I was here last January walking lost in my own thoughts when I suddenly realised an otter was calmly swimming along in the water just beside me. He dived sinuously several times before coming up to crunch on what looked to me like a rather un-appetising grisly sort of fish. After a while he got a bit fed up with me taking his picture and stopped to give me a menacing hiss, so I walked on and left him in peace.

Old bollard is a reminder of the past

Not so shy otter

The river goes on its way, but the path follows the canal

And they always tell you otters are so shy and elusive!

The Lagan itself is quite a river when you think about it, meandering for about 40 miles from its source on the slopes of Slieve Croob down near Dromara, taking a round-about course via Dromore and Moira before deciding to head for the city.

Work on the ambitious Lagan Navigation began in 1756 but the last stage was not completed until 1793. From Belfast to Lisburn the river was used with sections of canal to straighten the route on the wiggly bits. The canal then dropped down through ten locks to reach Lough Neagh.

It's difficult to visualise now how busy the waterway would have been in its heyday, providing both power and a means of transport for the many mills and factories on its banks. The barges were known as lighters and quite often the whole family actually lived on board and in 1893 it was recorded that they carried 150,000 tons of cargo on the canal.

However it was not to last. The arrival of the railways (the Belfast Lisburn line was opened in 1839) and improved roads saw a decline in traffic on the canal and the company which ran the canal, The Lagan Navigation Company, closed in 1954 followed shortly thereafter by the canal itself in 1958. Responsibility for the canal and towpath then passed to local government under whose auspices the Lagan Valley Regional Park was founded in 1967 under its first chairman, John Gilchrist who had been a long time campaigner to have the park established.

Part of a former lock

A little further on there is a disused footbridge, which I think is called Chimney Bridge for some reason, then the sound of rushing water reveals the location of the fifth lock. In all the times I walked the tow path I never thought about where the locks were situated until recently; so it was sort of like a game of spot the lock as generally there is not a lot left to see.

Next is, obviously, Lock 4 hidden under a bridge over to a picnic area

on a tiny island sandwiched between the river and the canal. Great spot for lunch accompanied by the roar of water cascading over the Eel Weir.

The towpath now rejoins the main river with Malone golf course visible on your other side. Cross over when you reach a brown painted footbridge, Gilchrist's Bridge presumably after the founder of the park, and carry on downstream.

At this point you have a choice to make. It time is tight or you don't feel up to it you can just carry on along the river omitting the loop to the Giant's Ring – but I don't recommend this as I think the Giant's ring is a fascinating place not to be missed and well worth the effort.

There is a track on the right at a National Trust sign for Minnowburn where there is also a very small red

Clockwise from top left: The Eel Weir; Canal towpath: The National Trust mark the way

arrow for Giant's Ring Trail on another post. The path takes you to the Edenderry road, across and through recently planted young beech

Glancing back at the snow capped Belfast Hills

trees, which will be wonderful when they are a bit bigger, and then across another road to a wooden gate. I love the coconut-like smell of the gorse bushes in the hedgerow when the sun hits them – somehow it's so redolent of lazy summer days; although the saying goes that there is always a whin

Edenderry village

bush blooming somewhere no matter what time of year it may be. Keep with the little red arrows and follow the gravel path between wire fences as it wends its way between rolling, well cultivated fields, ignoring a couple of stiles on the right leading off cross

Giant's Ring dolmen

country to Edenderry village nestling in a hollow.

Finally you come to the Ring. The exact purpose of this huge, imposing earth henge is lost in prehistory. Its design suggests it might have been used for ceremonial occasions and not

Walking round the Ring

to keep out enemies as the ditch is inside; it must have been an enormous undertaking when it was built, probably in the late Neolithic period. The passage tomb in the middle originally had a mound of earth over it and the cap stone has slipped but otherwise it remains much as it was

Farmland views from the top

Barnett's Park from Terrace Hill

out for a stile into a field, known as the Sandpit Field. I think the trail route just goes this way to take you off the road, the main feature is a big scoop in the land made by glaciation. You circle round the dips near the hedge, locating the next stile in the mud to come back out onto the same road a bit further along. On the other side of the road proceed through two gates and up an old tarmac drive on to Terrace Hill for a look at the rose gardens and the view over to grand Malone House, it's worth it even in winter. At one time Edward Robinson of Robinson and Cleaver owned Terrace Hill House, which is not open to the public, and the garden was part of his estate.

built; when there were several rings probably of wooden posts, around it. Other finds nearby indicate the area, Ballynahatty townland, was a centre for ritual activity at that time. You can walk round the top of the ring and get an impressive panorama of the Belfast Hills and surrounding countryside, possibly following in the footsteps of stone age people as they gathered to watch whatever took place below.

There is another gap at the far side of the Ring bringing you out through the car park; when you come to the road cross and walk to the left a bit looking

There are lots of carved wooden sculptures around this area, backtrack slightly and take the path near the one like a totem pole, down through the woods. The path forks and the right-hand branch leads near a pond with more sculptures (including one which to my eye looks like a bear

Minnowburn bridge

Old Shaw's Bridge

with glasses) but either will take you to the Minnowburn River; follow it downstream a short way until you reach the bridge and car park.

Saunter over the bridge and across the lane past a little blue marker saying The Meadows to rejoin the Lagan's right bank. On the opposite side the lawns of Barnett's Demesne, given to the city by the last tenant of Malone House, sweep down to the river. Soon Shaw's Bridge comes into view. The last in a series of bridges built here it's named after Cromwellian, Captain Shaw who had a strong oak version constructed for troops to cross, but the stone one is of a later date and may be

Hungry heron

The Red Bridge

made from stones from a nearby fort. The newer road bridge does not have the same charm…

After going under the bridge the path follows another stretch of canal which is well silted up with wonderful emerald green slime but again good for wildlife. That heron must be catching something in there!

This stretch is usually quite bustling with walkers because it is near the Lock Keeper's Cottage where there is information and a coffee shop. This bit unusually has an intact lock and bridge, the third or McLeave's lock. Just past it is the Red Bridge and

An idyllic summer Lagan

Nearing Stranmillis

Alternative path

The walkway follows the river into the city

Apartments line the far bank

The lifting bridge

you are back on the Lagan itself for a stretch.

A choice of paths now opens up at the next section of canal: the main tarmac one, a little dirt path on the other side of a footbridge or a loop round on the far Belvoir Forest side of the river. I generally opt for the middle one which is another wildlife friendly sylvan spot.

After this we are back across the next wee bridge and on the main river again as it widens. I've seen a seal in the water on this stretch near Lagan Meadows and I've heard they have even been seen up as far as Shaw's bridge, which must be a good sign of the state of the river – don't know why it was swimming upside down, though…

The river seems very dark and tranquil here just before you reach the real start of the city where the various boat clubs and the Cutter's Wharf pub force you to abandon the bank for a little way. Once through the car park follow signs for cycle route 9 beside some apartments, back along the waterside and by a mysterious sculpture called Homage to the Lagan.

The cycle route brings you under a road bridge and follows Stranmillis Embankment, yes it is a road but there are trees! Apparently Stranmillis means sweet stream which must have been open to question at times. Passing the refurbished Lyric Theatre and an entrance to the Botanic Gardens tells you you are nearly on the home stretch. Once past the Ormeau Bridge you find a paved walkway with the river still on your right. I find strolling along here quite enjoyable in a different sort of way, there are so many reminders of the story of the city past and present.

The structure in the river here is

Waterfront Hall

The Lagan Weir

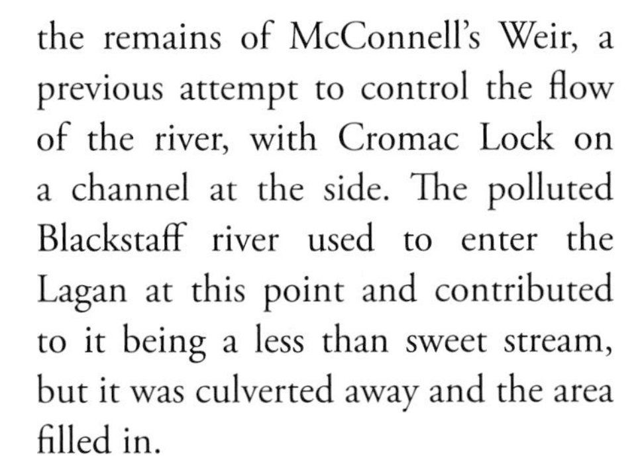

the remains of McConnell's Weir, a previous attempt to control the flow of the river, with Cromac Lock on a channel at the side. The polluted Blackstaff river used to enter the Lagan at this point and contributed to it being a less than sweet stream, but it was culverted away and the area filled in.

There is a staggered barrier leading to the bottom entrance of Central Station across a grassy area near here, if you want to cut a bit off the walk. Otherwise the foot and cycle way carries on and crosses over the little lifting bridge. Between the apartment blocks with what look to me like strange ears on the top you get your first glimpse of two of Belfast's most familiar landmarks – the giant cranes known as Samson and Goliath. Built when Harland and Wolff were flourishing the cranes more or less went out of use with the decline in shipbuilding, as the yard concentrated on smaller engineering and construction projects. Worries that they might disappear from the skyline were allayed when they were scheduled as historic monuments.

Across the road at the end of Albert Bridge and the route leads under a another bridge and on towards the distinctive curved frontage of the

Statue of Harmony

Waterfront Hall, now unfortunately dwarfed by the Hilton and BT buildings. For some reason all the trees along here slope to the right, can't be that windy here surely. Moored alongside is the dutch barge 'Confiance' which has been turned into a maritime museum. Keep following the river past a well known sculpture, Nuala with the Hula or the Statue of Harmony as it is

New and old – the Titanic building and Harland and Wolff crane

The Big Fish

officially known. There is also a large display board with information about Sustrans cycle routes on one side and facts about the River Lagan on the other.

After crossing at the ends of the next two bridges; Queen's and Queen Elizabeth, you find yourself at the Lagan Weir, built in 1994 to control the flow of water between tides. Prior to this the when the tide was low it could leave exposed mud flats as far up as the Ormeau Embankment. An information board tells you about the rebirth of the river and return of wildlife due to the construction of the weir in 1994. The river and weir look particularly attractive at night with the lights reflecting in the water, I love looking down on it from the train as it crosses over.

It's worth pausing a minute to have a closer look at the Big Fish sculpture if you haven't before. Sculptor John Kindness used themes from the history of the town and contributions from local children as designs for the many ceramic tiles covering the fish. He was also influenced by the idea that around here is where one of Belfast's hidden rivers, the Farset, joins the Lagan. This is really where the city had its beginnings at a sandbank or ford in the river, giving Belfast its name. A few years ago a documentary shown on TV about stabilising the Albert Clock (the original foundations of the clock appeared to be four tree trunks stuck into sludge so I'm glad they got that sorted!) made me realise just how much history is hidden under the streets of our modern city.

Nearby is the departure point for boat tours round the harbour and as you proceed look out for the Titanic building glimpsed below the motorway bridge. Most people are really enthusiastic about this and it is impressive but I'm not so sure – I still think it looks like four cheese graters joined at the corners!

Before this area, Queen's Island, became part of the docks it was a park and pleasure ground separated by a channel from the rest of the harbour. The island itself was formed from reclaimed land when the channel into the port was dredged so that larger ships could use it. Previously known as Dargan's Island it cost a penny to cross over to by boat. The attractions included flower gardens and bathing huts and public events such as balloon ascents took place there. It just shows how people's taste in entertainment has changed over the years.

Before the construction of the channel the larger ships had to transfer their cargoes to small boats three miles away from the quays at the end

'Dividers' sculpture with Obel building in the background

of High Street or Waring Street. At low tide steamers were stuck near Whitehouse and men with wee boats would row out and offer to bring passengers up to the town for a shilling, quite expensive considering they packed in as many as they could.

After passing the bottom of the twenty eight story Obel building, Belfast's tallest, keep with the cycle route signs as you come up to the road and go under the bridge into Corporation Square and turn right through a vehicle barrier. On the Harbour Commissioner's Office there is a blue plaque in honour of ship builder William Richie, and in fact the modern extension to the building is named after him.

Until I saw this plaque I hadn't heard of Richie so I looked him up. He and his brother had come over from Scotland and started a successful business in the last decade of the 18th century. His shipyard was where the square is now but the dry dock still survives. Hugh Richie joined up with Alexander McLaine to form the Richie & McLaine ship building yard which went on to build the 'Belfast', the first steam ship made in Ireland. I don't know why we don't plug these successes more instead of the Titanic, which after all was a tragic disaster.

Clarendon graving docks

The Flying Angel

The route now takes you through Clarendon Dock Business Park, with various maritime artworks and yet another information board giving details. It goes over two wee footbridges, one of them crossing the original dry dock, and cuts through the red brick buildings so watch out for our old friend, the cycle route sign, ahead. Wind your way among the new blocks along the tree lined roadway made from square setts, the signs then direct you through a tall gate into a car park, half reserved for the Mission to Seafarers. There is a really striking sculpture here by artist Maurice Harron of the mission's Flying Angel symbol. In the road there are the remains of railway lines dating from the time this area was the centre of dockland activity. Although life was hard for the sailors, dock workers and their families (or perhaps because it was), around these terraced streets known as Sailortown, there developed a strong community where different faiths and nationalities mingled. Although the area suffered during the Belfast Blitz, it was the radical changes in the shipping industry in the latter decades of the twentieth century which heralded the decline of this community before redevelopment for the construction of the motorway finally finished it off.

After this it's just a case of crossing the road and following the white line labelled with cycle/walk signs round into Garmoyle Street. Swing left past the fire station and cross Duncrue Street. If you detour a bit right to the corner you will spot the chimney of Jennymount Mill further along across the motorway-one of the few survivors left of the numerous mills in the city, although the Lanyon designed building is now offices. There seems to be a haunting associated with old Jennymount, a possibly headless horseman known as Galloper Thompson so watch out if you hear the hoof beats of his ghostly steed… then back track and dive through the subway under the motorway to come out into the car park at Yorkgate Station.

Stormont Drive

Stormont to Holywood

START: CAR PARK JUST PAST MAIN ENTRANCE TO STORMONT
FINISH: HOLYWOOD RAILWAY STATION
HOW LONG: ABOUT 11KM/7 MILES
TYPE OF WALK: PARKS AND COUNTRY ROADS WITH ONE BUSIER SECTION
PUBLIC TRANSPORT: METRO BUS 4A/B TO STORMONT, BANGOR LINE TRAIN TO HOLYWOOD. (IF YOU ARE DOING THIS WALK IN ONE DIRECTION USING PUBLIC TRANSPORT TO AND FROM BELFAST IS BEST)

Although the Craigantlet hills through which this walk passes might not be regarded by locals as part of the 'Belfast Hills', for any visitor standing in the centre of Belfast looking around, they are very much part of the chain of hills which encircle the city and I feel a rural circumnavigation of the city would be incomplete without this dander up past Northern Ireland's seat of government and on over the hill to enjoy a unique panorama of the city.

Starting from the car park near the play area beyond the main Stormont entrance, go up to the right past an enclosed picnic area and then along the fence of the sports pitches on the other side. The right hand path circles round the Wetlands Project area where you can use the boardwalk if it is open to get right into the wetland (if it's not open just go on round). A board tells of the plans for this project, involving encouraging native trees, clearing ponds and encouraging birds.

Boardwalk through the wetlands

You now emerge at a small toilet block where you could cut across the main approach to Stormont and simply take one of the little paths up through the woods to the side gate from Massey Avenue. Alternatively head on up the drive towards Stormont Buildings, to the right you can get a glimpse through the trees of the older baronial style Stormont Castle, occupied by the first ministers

Stormont Castle

office and department. A more modest house was originally on the site, known as Storm Mount, which came to the Reverend John Clelland on his marriage. Clelland was Rector of Newtownards and employed variously as tutor and agent by the Castlereagh family and acted as magistrate, a position he seems to have used to keep the district under his control. Getting hold of more land and money by some rather suspect means the family had the place rebuilt on a grand scale. The new castle, designed by local architect Thomas Turner, included an enormous ballroom, now in use as a cabinet room. Alas, it can only be viewed by the public on the two heritage open days.

As you cross in front of Stormont itself pause to admire the vista down the other way. From the road the driveway looks to dip down before rising up to Carson's statue but walking up here you soon realise that this is an optical illusion and that it's just various grades of uphill all the way! You so often see pictures of the building but because of the elevation there is a wonderful sweep across the city outskirts to the Castlereagh hills visible from the steps in front. There must be a great view from the windows – what a pity the people inside must be far too busy to appreciate it!

Although constructed comparatively recently, opening in 1932, Stormont is neoclassical in style – designed to impress by Sir Arnold Thornley. Unfortunately the gleaming Portland stone exterior has never been quite the same since

Stormont buildings

it was painted to camouflage it during the war. I think some of the pictures you see must be air-brushed; I once went for a walk there in the snow and the building definitely did look slightly dingy against the white. However it still makes quite a statement, helped also by the layout of the grounds.

On the far side of the buildings there is a very pleasant detour if you turn up hill to the right past the Reconciliation statue and through the woods to the top of the lovely peaceful glen with its wee bridge. Continuing down again through the trees on the other side of the little tumbling stream, you pass another statue known as The Gleaner; made for the 1951 Festival of Britain but somehow reminding me of the kind of thing they made in 1930s Russia in its

The Gleaner

solidity and emphasis on the value of hard work. A little further down there are some trees with a plaque dedicating them to the fallen at the Battle of the Somme.

Exit this time at the gate and barriers into Massey Avenue. As you pass spare a glance at poor Netherleigh house, a handsome Georgian style mansion home to several government

Quiet glen above Stormont

Distant Campbell College

departments. The house is built on what was part of the old Belmont Estate and has had a chequered career, including use as a convalescent hospital for American soldiers in the war and housing Campbell College's sports club. Probably by Lynn of Lanyon, Lynn and Lanyon, unfortunately the house had horrible red brick extensions stuck onto it during refurbishment in 1976.

At the end of the avenue turn right up Belmont Road and keep on for a mile or so taking care on a short section where there is no pavement. At some point the Belmont Road disappears into a side road and the main route becomes the Ballymiscaw Road and though quite busy starts to feel more like the country as you pull up onto the hill. A panorama spreads out behind you of with the red tower of Campbell College standing out. It's a bit of a relief to turn left when you reach quiet Moss Road at the top of the hill.

There is a wonderful panorama of the Belfast Hills displayed on your left soon after you start walking along here, and rolling, fertile fields all around as you move further up.

Where the track divides bear right and head past a farmhouse with barking dogs; the track branches left and rejoins the more surfaced road so bend your path to the

Rolling fields above Holywood

Entrance to Moss Road

Looking over towards the city from Moss Road in summer…

...and winter

right again. I realised how exposed it really is here during the heavy snow we had in 2013 when I turned this corner and found the track blocked by a snowdrift taller than me! They had cleared the lane most of the way but must have been forced to give up at this point. I followed some footsteps which cut across an empty field on the corner and found it was possible to clamber over the lower levels of snow beyond the drift, but the house whose entrance gates are just here was really cut off.

As you head downhill striking views open up on both sides, out to the lough and down over Holywood. Eventually you come out at some big gate posts with a sign saying

Holywood comes into view

Glenlyon Park, another path to explore

Sunlight dapples the water in Glenlyon

'pedestrian access only' on the other side; not much use to motorists when there's nothing at the other end of the road to indicate this!

Make your way left along the road looking out for a wooden barrier at a gap in the fence on the other side. This brings you to some steps leading into Glenlyon park. If you have the energy you can explore up this little gem of a glen, or just turn left and then right at the next junction. Stroll down another little path on the left and through the car park and you are on Church Road which leads down into Holywood.

If you want another pleasing little diversion turn right into Church Avenue and follow it round a couple of corners to a footpath sneaking between the houses and along the stream to Twisel Bridge. Hidden in behind the buildings this pretty little nook was created in 1912 in appreciative memory of a local man and was also known as The Kissing Bridge. When emerging at the far end I like to swing right up the road, rather than heading into the town, and cross over the next road to go down Woodlands. At the bottom is Ballymenoch Park and you can pick a path through the 20 acre wooded parkland heading for the bottom left hand corner near the main road. It needs a bit of care crossing the dual carriageway but at least you can do it in two goes, then

Ballymenoch Park;

The coastal path leads you towards Holywood

a short stroll down Seapark Road takes you to the grassy recreation area on the lough shore. Heading left will bring you back towards Holywood with several subways that will get you to the far side of the railway tracks and up to the train station, or into the town itself.

NI Countryside Code

The walks in this book are mostly on public parkland but observing a few simple guidelines will enhance the pleasure of being out in the open air, both for yourself and others

Respect the people who live and work in the countryside
Show courtesy and consideration to everybody. Be a friendly visitor with a responsible manner.

Know where you are allowed to go
Most land is private property and access is only available with the goodwill and tolerance of the owner. Whilst most landowners do not object to recreational users on their land, some do. Always comply with a landowner's wishes.

Keep to paths across farmland
Help prevent damage to crops by walking around the edge of a field unless there is an existing path across it. Avoid fields where there are animals, as your presence may cause them stress and endanger your own safety.

Use gates and stiles to cross fences, hedges and walls
When crossing fences, hedges and walls, use the nearest gate or stile. Damage to fencing can allow animals to stray. If you must climb a gate because it is difficult to open, always do this at the hinged end.

Leave gates as you find them
If you find a gate closed, close it when you pass through to prevent animals straying. Farmers sometimes leave gates open to allow animals to pass from one field to another to graze or drink. Help a farmer by leaving gates as you find them, but if in doubt, do close a gate.

Do not interfere with livestock, machinery and crops
These are valuable commodities and should be left alone. Interference with animals and equipment may endanger you. Pay attention to warning signs as they are there for your protection.

Keep dogs under control
Keep your dog on a lead when walking on roads or when close to farm animals. A dog can cause distress to animals and endanger you. Keep your dog under control at all times so as not to disturb wildlife or annoy other visitors.

Keep all water sources clean
The public water supply is not available to everyone living in the countryside. Take care with your personal hygiene and do not pollute water. Don't interfere with water troughs which provide clean water for livestock.

Protect wildlife plants and trees
Leave all natural places as you find them. Never uproot plants as they will be lost forever. Keep your distance from wild birds and animals to prevent disturbance and stress especially to adults that are with young and in winter when food may be scarce or weather harsh.

Take your litter home
All litter is unsightly. Glass, tins and plastic bags can be dangerous to people, livestock and wildlife. Keep the countryside clean by taking home your own litter and any which you may come across.

Guard against all risk of fire
The countryside is vulnerable to fire especially during dry weather. Accidental fires pose a great risk to farmers and foresters. Be careful to extinguish all used matches and cigarettes. Use a stove for cooking rather than a fire. Never throw cigarettes from a car window.

Make no unnecessary noise
One of the attractions of the countryside is its peace and quiet. Do not disturb this with noise or disruptive behaviour which might annoy residents and visitors or frighten farm animals and wildlife.

Respect other recreational users
Behave responsibly. Where possible, warn others of your approach and slow down or stop if necessary. Irresponsible behaviour could lead to you and your activity being banned from the area in the future.

Take special care on country roads
Always drive carefully with reduced speed on country roads. Consider others when parking and avoid blocking entrances, gateways or other drivers' visibility. Walkers should take special care on narrow country roads and if appropriate, walk in single file.

Consider your personal safety
If possible do not go alone. Wear suitable clothing and footwear as the weather can change very quickly. Don't go if the weather conditions are beyond your experience.

For more information and to see our other titles, please visit our website
www.cottage-publications.com
or alternatively you can contact us as follows:–

Telephone: +44 (0)28 9188 8033
Fax: +44 (0)28 9188 8063

Cottage Publications
is an imprint of
Laurel Cottage Ltd.,
15 Ballyhay Road,
Donaghadee, Co. Down,
N. Ireland, BT21 0NG